PRAYER &
BAND TOPICS

CHRISTIAN CONCEPTS FOR GROWTH AND DEVELOPMENT

THE SEAL OF THE CHURCH OF GOD IN CHRIST, INC.
ORGANIZED 1907
MEMPHIS, TENNESSEE

FALL QUARTER 2015
SEPTEMBER-OCTOBER-NOVEMBER

CHURCH OF GOD IN CHRIST, INC.
PRAYER & BIBLE BAND TOPICS
FALL QUARTER SEPTEMBER • OCTOBER • NOVEMBER 2015

Bishop Charles E. Blake, Sr.
Presiding Bishop

Superintendent Mark A. Ellis, D.Div.
Chairman, Publishing Board

Paperback : ISBN–10: 1680870270   ISBN–13: 978–1–68087–027–5
eBook : ISBN–10: 1680870289   ISBN–13: 978–1–68087–028–2

The Prayer & Bible Band Topics Volume 53 Number 1 is published quarterly by
The Church Of God In Christ Publishing House
2500 Lamar Avenue • Memphis, TN 38114

Table Of Contents

THE GUIDE FOR WEEKLY BIBLE BAND MEETINGS

For weekly Bible Band meetings, the President should plan each meeting one week in advance.

- Secure a leader for devotion who will make preparations.

- Meetings should never last longer than two hours; however, let the Spirit of God lead.

- Appoint a different spiritual minded individual for the leader of the devotional service.

ORDER OF SERVICE

- Call to Order (by the President)
- Singing
- Prayer
- Scripture Devotional Reading
- A Five Minute Talk (on the devotion by the leader)
- President's Remarks
- President presents the teacher
- Announcements and Remarks
- Singing
- Benediction

Letter From
The Presiding Bishop

To All Students of the Word of God and Diligent Workers,

It is an honor and privilege to address you in these Quarterly lessons. It is in the Quarterly curriculums that we learn the Word of God, discuss the lessons for knowledge and growth, and we come together as a community. Curriculums are a living, breathing community all on their own within the church, breathing new life, revelation, and friendships. These powerful lessons will teach us the importance of praying for one another the power of sharing our gifts and talents with each other to enhance the Kingdom of God, and, most of all, the way we are to bring our communities together.

The tragic events of Ferguson, New York, and Baltimore all show that we must engage our communities around our local churches with prayer for hurting families, with fasting to break the chains of injustice for all people, and with the love and power of the Word of God to show that we are stronger together with God in our lives. My appeal to you, as the Presiding Bishop of this Great Church (the Church Of God In Christ, Inc.), is that we stand together united in love, prayer, and fasting and with the compassion of God. It was through God's compassion that we were created, that He gave us Jesus Christ to save us from our sins, and that we have been given the Word of God to live by.

I would like to thank the the Church Of God In Christ Publishing Board and the Publishing House for their continued work and dedication to the Saints of God. Thanks to the International Departments who continually keep our literature as their resource curriculum of choice. Thanks so much to this fine team who have shown that they are extremely committed to excellence in the Word of God.

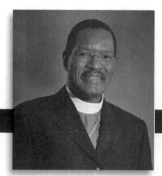

Bishop Charles E. Blake, Sr.
Presiding Bishop
Church Of God In Christ, Inc.
Seventh in Succession

Letter From
The Chairman Of The Board

Greetings to the People of God,

What a blessing it is to know that we have a God on our side who not only looks out for us, but also shares with us His love and kindness and imparts His wisdom in us! Yet, what good does it do for us to not spread that love and kindness among our brothers and sisters? What good does it do us for us to withhold that godly wisdom from our friends, families, and, more importantly, our community. A physical structure is merely a building that has been dedicated to the glory of God. However, the true church is the people of God; the people of God who willingly share the teachings and laws of God with others.

It is through love and kindness that He has drawn us. It is through that same love and that same kindness that we draw and engage our community. It's our time to come alive in the body of Christ! Why? Just as Jesus Christ is yet alive, He requires that same Spirit of life to be alive in us. It is that same spirit of liveliness that will determine if we go back with Him when He comes again; we must bring not only ourselves, but also our community with us. Our Lord and Savior Jesus Christ is not selfish, and He definitely demands that we become just like Him.

I encourage every reader to become extremely committed to the Word of God and get into this quarter with excitement and expectation as we break down the Scriptures.

Thank you so much for believing in the Church Of God In Christ Publishing House. Come and join me in this journey this quarter.

Superintendent Mark A. Ellis
Chairman of the Publishing Board
Church Of God In Christ, Inc.

Letter From
The Chairman Of Marketing

To All Students and Workers of Christ Jesus,

I am excited to address you each and every time in our Quarterly Lessons. I believe that the study of the Word of God is vital to each department within our church. It is through the knowledge we gain as we study that we can learn how to bring unity and the knowledge of God to the forefront of our communities. It is in building up our communities that show that we are diligent workers of Christ—that we are extremely committed to building the Kingdom of God. The events that we see reported daily indicate to believers that Jesus is soon to return. We must be found working, showing love to one another and to those in our communities.

Jesus Christ spoke only a few times in the synagogue, but the majority of His sermons were preached outside of the city to accommodate the people. The only way that we can truly show the love of Christ and the grace of God is by engaging the Christian community and energizing it to come alive in love, power, and authority. To do this, we must come together for one another—that's the love; we must trust in the Holy Ghost that He is working on our behalf—that's the power; and we must know that the Spirit is "not for sale"—that's the authority.

We, the members of the Church Of God In Christ body, are stronger together, and our communities need us just like we need them. For Jesus Christ is getting us ready for His second coming, and what better way to be prepared than by working in our local communities.

Many thanks to the Saints of God, the Church Of God In Christ Publishing Board, and the Publishing House for their continued dedication to the Word and work of the Lord. Thanks to all of the Departments and Churches across the country for their loyal support of the Church Of God In Christ's literature. As always, let me personally thank each of you for your continued support and encouragement by purchasing the curriculums. Remember, without you, this dream wouldn't have become a reality; and "a church without its people is just an empty shell."

Yours for service,
Evangelist Sandra Smith Jones
Chairman of Marketing – Publishing Board
Church Of God In Christ, Inc.

PREFACE

'I do not believe that any man can preach the gospel who does not preach the Law. The Law is the needle, and you cannot draw the silken thread of the gospel through a man's heart unless you first send the needle of the Law to make way for it. If men do not understand the Law, they will not feel they are sinners. And if they are not consciously sinners, they will never value the sin offering. There is no healing a man till the Law has wounded him, no making him alive till the Law has slain him." Charles Spurgeon

Most of us feel uncomfortable when someone who has done something for us continually reminds us of that special gesture. We are appreciative, but we don't want to feel beholden to anyone. We don't want to be made to feel as though we owe them anything more than a debt of gratitude. If we aren't careful, that same way of thinking can affect how we think about God and His right to command our obedience and worship. God has the right to dictate what we are to think, how we are to behave, how we are to dress, what we are to say, where we are to go, with whom we are to associate, and what we are to do because He is not our handiwork, but we are His. Those of us who are parents have the right to expect our children to obey our rules, be loyal to our household, uphold our family values, etc. If we as imperfect beings have the right to demand complete obedience from our children, how much more does our perfectly holy and righteous Father have the right to demand the same from us?

In this series of lessons, we will take another look at the Ten Commandments. The Ten Commandments have served as the foundation of moral and judicial codes in civilized nations throughout the world, from ancient times until now. Just as organizations, such the American Civil Liberties Union, have fought vigorously to remove public displays of the Ten Commandments from schools and court rooms and council chambers throughout this nation, we as believers must also fight vigorously to proclaim the timeless truths which have greatly influenced the moral fabric of our country and our lives.

Exodus 19:1–9, 21–24

Our Agreement To Enter Into Covenant Relationship

Central Verse

"Now therefore, if ye will obey my voice indeed, and keep my covenant, then ye shall be a peculiar treasure unto me above all people: for all the earth is mine." **Exodus 19:5, KJV**

"Now if you obey me fully and keep my covenant, then out of all nations you will be my treasured possession. Although the whole earth mine." **Exodus 19:5, N**

Devotional Reading

Genesis 17:1–9

Key Terms

Sinai – "Thorny"; the mountain where Moses received the Law from Jehovah; located at the southern end of the Sinai peninsula between the horns of the Red Sea; exact site unknown.

Covenant – Alliance, pledge, agreement.

Peculiar treasure – Possession, property; valued property.

Sanctify – To consecrate, prepare, dedicate, be hallowed, be holy, be sanctified, be separate.

Break forth – To break through or down or over, burst, breach.

Introduction

Before God gave Moses and the Children of Israel t Ten Commandments, He reminded them of three thing the miraculous works He performed on their beha including the defeat of the Egyptians; His great love f them and how He chose them above all the nations the earth; and finally, of His plans for them to becom *"a kingdom of priests and a holy nation"* (verse 6). Th not only laid the foundation for their faith, but also f their obedience.

Discussion

God knew Israel would be tempted to forsake Hi during their journey. He knew they would be tempt to follow the example of the heathen peoples they wou encounter. He knew their hearts even as they fell their faces and promised to obey Him. Rememberi what God had done for them and how special the were to Him should have helped them remain faith to Him. The same is true for believers today. Israe experiences during their journey are similar to situatio we face today. They are marvelous examples of Go grace. They demonstrate that we can have complete confidence in God to meet our nee and know that He truly cares for us. Remembering past victories during current trials a reflecting on God's love can help us remain steadfast.

And the LORD said unto Moses, Lo, I come unto thee in a thick cloud, that the people may hear when I speak with thee, and believe thee for ever. And Moses told the words of the people unto the LORD.

And the LORD said unto Moses, Go down, charge the people, lest they break through unto the LORD to gaze, and many of them perish.

And let the priests also, which come near to the LORD, sanctify themselves, lest the LORD break forth upon them.

And Moses said unto the LORD, The people cannot come up to mount Sinai: for thou chargedst us, saying, Set bounds about the mount, and sanctify it.

And the LORD said unto him, Away, get thee down, and thou shalt come up, thou, and Aaron with thee: but let not the priests and the people break through to come up unto the LORD, lest he break forth upon them (Exodus 19:9, 21–24).

God's presence was hidden in a thick cloud. Only Moses and his brother Aaron had the privilege of touching God's holy mountain, Mount Sinai. The rest of the people gathered at the base of Mount Sinai and that was after having been consecrated and their clothes washed. Anyone who dared to transgress this command was to be shot through with an arrow or stoned to death from a distance. The people witnessed a sight that was both awesome and terrible in its display. Holy fire and smoke engulfed the entire mountain. They heard the loud rumblings and saw the brilliant flashes of lightning. They saw the fiery blaze and the thick, heavy smoke. They felt the ground move beneath their feet as Mount Sinai shook.

Conclusion

Can you imagine what the Children of Israel saw and how they felt at that terrible moment? What will it be like for us to meet God if we have not been faithful to Him and to His Word? This was the question that the Children of Israel had to ponder standing at the base of Mount Sinai then and the same question we have to answer as we stand at the foot of Christ's Cross. Israel couldn't be known as God's people just because God called them special. They had to demonstrate their position in Him through their obedience to His Word. The Ten Commandments formed the basis of the rules governing the covenant relationship between God and His people. The covenant was not forced upon them at that time, just as it is not forced upon anyone today. The Children of Israel had to agree to obey God. We also have to agree to obey God. We make this agreement when we confess the Lord Jesus Christ as our personal Savior.

Questions:

1. Why was it necessary to sanctify the people before they gathered at Mount Sinai to witness the presence of God there?

2. Why did God recite the history of His involvement with the children of Israel before giving Moses the Ten Commandments? What was He trying to establish?

_____

_____

3. What identifies us as Christians today? Is there a sharp distinction between us and the rest of the world or has our identity become muddled and confused?

_____

_____

4. How does remembering God's grace and goodness help us remain faithful to Him? Are they the only reasons we should exercise faith in Him?

_____

_____

 *Essential* THOUGHT   "We are in covenant relationship with God. Our obedience to God separates us from the rest of the world."

missed lesson

Exodus 20:1–6; 2 Corinthians 6:14–18

God Does Not Share His Glory

Central Verses

"I am the LORD thy God, which have brought thee out of the land of Egypt, out of the house of bondage. Thou shalt have no other gods before me."
Exodus 20:2 – 3, KJV

"I am the LORD your God, who brought you out of Egypt, out of the land of slavery. You shall have no other gods before me."
Exodus 20: 2 – 3, NIV

Devotional Reading

Leviticus 26:8–13

Key Terms

graven image – Idol

jealous – Intolerant of rivalry or unfaithfulness.

Belial – "Worthless or wicked"; a name of Satan.

unequally yoked – 1. To come under an unequal or different yoke; 2. have fellowship with one who is not an equal: 2 Cor. 6:14, where the Apostle is forbidding Christians to have intercourse with idolaters.

Introduction

Scholars believe that idolatry originated from man's enthrallment with God's creation. As humans looked upon its beauty and splendor, their minds *"would soon pass from admiration to reverence and worship. Thus homage would be paid to the sun, moon, and stars, which was only due to the Creator. The reverence felt for men of genius gave them an ideal grandeur, and exalted them to the rank of deities"* (Exell, p. 350). Some authors include both of these commandments as one. To do so is to miss an important distinction between idolatry and the worship of images. Idolatry as it is forbidden by the First Commandment is *"the worship of false gods,"* while the Second Commandment specifically addresses the worship of *"images or representations of the true God"* (Exell, p. 350). These acts will only have the effect of turning *"aside the mind from God"* (Exell, p. 350).

Discussion

Again, God reminds Israel that He brought them out of the land of Egypt and delivered them from the miseries and abuses they suffered as slaves to the Egyptians. What He could not deliver them from was the influence of the polytheistic ancient Egyptian culture generations of Hebrews grew up in. The ancient Egyptians worshipped thousands of gods, as many as 1500 to 2000 or more, so there was a god for practically everything. God delivered Israel from bondage to men, but their obedience to Him would have to come from their own volition. They would have to be willing to forsake idolatry not only in the physical sense, but in the spiritual as well. Why? Because God does not share His glory:

"I am the LORD: that is my name: and my glory will I not give to another, neither my praise to graven images" (Isaiah 42:8).

> *Be ye not unequally yoked together with unbelievers: for what fellowship hath righteousness with unrighteousness? and what communion hath light with darkness?*
> *And what concord hath Christ with Belial? or what part hath he that believeth with an infidel?*
> *And what agreement hath the temple of God with idols? for ye are the temple of the living God; as God hath said, I will dwell in them, and walk in them; and I will be their God, and they shall be my people. Wherefore come out from among them, and be ye separate, saith the Lord, and touch not the unclean thing; and I will receive you. And will be a Father unto you, and ye shall be my sons and daughters, saith the Lord Almighty* (2 Corinthians 6: 14 – 18).

Conclusion

Idol worship wasn't only a problem for the Hebrews of the Old Testament. Paul appealed to the Corinthians to break away from idolatry. He meant the worship of idols as well as the evil influences of worldliness and the flesh. As believers, we are in covenant relationship and covenant partnership with God. Not all relationships and partnerships are beneficial. As temples of the Living God, we do not covenant with false gods. We do not glorify anything or anyone other than our Father. God will not allow us to give His glory to anyone or anything else without severe consequences following.

Questions:

1. What is the distinction between the First and Second Commandments? Discuss how Isaiah 42:8 supports this distinction.

   _____

   _____

2. What does God mean when He describes Himself as *jealous*? How does that compare and contrast with man's definition and use of the word?

   _____

   _____

Essential
THOUGHT   "Whatever occupies our hearts, minds, and time most is our idol."

Exodus 20:7; Joshua 23:6–8

Misusing God's Name

Central Verse

Thou shalt not take the name of the LORD thy God in vain; for the LORD will not hold him guiltless that taketh his name in vain."

Exodus 20:7, KJV

"You shall not misuse the name of the LORD your God, for the LORD will not hold anyone guiltless who misuses his name."

Exodus 20:7, NIV

Devotional Reading
Deuteronomy 10:19–22

Key Terms

in vain – Emptiness, vanity, falsehood; a) nothingness; b) emptiness of speech, lying; c) worthlessness of conduct).

guiltless – To be empty, be clear, be pure, be free, be innocent, be desolate, be cut off.

swear – To take an oath.

cleave – To cling, stick, stay close, keep close, stick to, stick with, follow closely, join to, overtake, catch.

Introduction

On January 7th of this year, Islamic terrorists stormed into the offices of the French satirical publication, *Charlie Hebdo*. They gunned down 22 persons—11 of whom were killed. The attack was motivated by cartoons which belittled their prophet. It was a shocking and senseless act of violence, yet it did little to educate the antireligious world on how an irreverent and offensive depiction of a religious figure can be deemed so deeply offensive.

Discussion

Why is it important to understand why God issued this commandment concerning the use of His name? Author Reverend John Exell explained it this way: *"By the name of God is often understood God Himself; for to call on God's name and on Himself are one"* (Exell, p. 353). This means that misusing or abusing God's name equals misusing or abusing God Himself—that is, God's person is not separated from His name. It is a form of blasphemy. God is Holy, and so is His name.

What does it mean to take the name of the Lord in vain? Exodus 20:7 in the Amplified version provides clarity: *"You shall not use or repeat the name of the Lord your God in vain [that is, lightly or frivolously, in false affirmations or profanely]; for the Lord will not hold him guiltless who takes His name in vain."* Taking God's name in vain not only covers all manner of swearing (especially when swearing that something false is true), vulgarity, profanity, disrespect, carelessness, and improper use of His name.

7

Be ye therefore very courageous to keep and to do all that is written in the book of the law of Moses, that ye turn not aside therefrom to the right hand or to the left; That ye come not among these nations, these that remain among you; neither make mention of the name of their gods, nor cause to swear by them, neither serve them, nor bow yourselves unto them: But cleave unto the LORD your God, as ye have done unto this day (Joshua 23:6 – 8).

Conclusion

At this time, God had given Israel rest from their battles with their enemies as they fought to possess the Promised Land. There was land yet to be taken. To be victorious, the people had to remain obedient to God and careful concerning their covenant with Him. Advanced in years, Joshua was about to die and in his farewell address to the leaders of the people of Israel, he reminded them of their duty to cleave to God. This included not lifting up the names of the gods of the heathen inhabitants who remained among them. To do so would ascribe to their false gods the glory that rightly belongs to the Living God. As Hannah put it, *"Whatever makes Him less than supreme, less than all–power, all–wisdom, all–love, is taking His name in vain. To attribute any real power, authority, or dominion to anything or anyone else, is taking His name in vain"* (Hannah, 1899).

Questions:

1. What does taking the Lord's name in vain mean to you? Discuss other passages of Scripture concerning the holiness of and reverence due God's name.

_____

_____

2. Compared with deities of other faiths, is the name of God more or less abused?

_____

_____

3. Using God's name in vulgarity and profanity is clearly understood, but what does it mean to use God's name lightly and frivolously? Why is this equally as prohibited as using His name in swearing and profanity?

_____

_____

Essential THOUGHT "God's name is Holy and is to be reverenced. He will punish those who take His name in vain."

Exodus 20:8–11; Matthew 12:1–14

Keeping The Sabbath Holy

Central Verses

Remember the sabbath day, to keep it holy. Six days shalt thou labour, and do all thy work: but the seventh day is the sabbath of the LORD thy God: in it thou shalt not do any work, thou, nor thy son, nor thy daughter, thy manservant, nor thy maidservant, nor thy cattle, nor thy stranger that is within thy gates."

Exodus 20:8–10, KJV

"Remember the Sabbath day by keeping it holy. Six days you shall labor and do all your work, but the seventh day is a sabbath to the LORD your God. On it you shall not do any work, neither you, nor your son or daughter, nor your male or female servant, nor your animals, nor any foreigner residing in your towns."

Exodus 20:8–10 NIV

Devotional Reading

Isaiah 56:1–7

Key Terms

Sabbath – a) The seventh day of the week observed from Friday evening to Saturday evening as a day of rest and worship by Jews and some Christians; b) Sunday observed among Christians as a day of rest and worship.

Rested – To rest, settle down and remain.

Lawful – Being in harmony with the law; constituted, authorized, or established by law.

Introduction

Sundays are among the busiest and potentially most lucrative days in the restaurant business, yet every Sunday, the more than 1480 restaurants in the Chick–fil–A chain are closed. In the company's mission statement, the practice is explained as giving employees a day to spend in worship, fellowship, and with family. The late founder of the restaurant chain, Truett Cathy, felt this policy was both an example of faithful stewardship and would also attract quality employees who cherished the same values. Cathy proved a business can be successful by allowing its employees time to spend in worship and with their families.

Discussion

In Judaism, the Sabbath begins at sundown on Friday and continues through sundown on Saturday. While the children of Israel sojourned in the wilderness, God provided a double–portion of manna prior to the beginning of the Sabbath, so that the people would not have to go out and gather it on that day as they did on the other six days of the week. Any manna leftover during the other weekdays drew worms and stank by morning, but not the manna God provided for the Sabbath. It did not corrupt. The manna was a miraculous blessing and the fact that the manna remained unspoiled for use for meals on the Sabbath was also a miracle.

There have been so many calendar changes over the centuries that it is difficult to know

9

with any certainty what day of the week is considered the Sabbath Day. What we do know is that the Sabbath was a covenant between God and His people. It was to serve as a reminder that God, after spending six days creating the world and all therein, rested from His labors. It was also to be a day of rest for servants – a reminder to Israel of how God delivered them from Egyptian bondage.

At that time Jesus went on the sabbath day through the corn; and his disciples were an hungred, and began to pluck the ears of corn and to eat.

But when the Pharisees saw it, they said unto him, Behold, thy disciples do that which is not lawful to do upon the sabbath day.

But he said unto them, Have ye not read what David did, when he was an hungred, and they that were with him;

How he entered into the house of God, and did eat the shewbread, which was not lawful for him to eat, neither for them which were with him, but only for the priests?

Or have ye not read in the law, how that on the sabbath days the priests in the temple profane the sabbath, and are blameless?

But I say unto you, That in this place is one greater than the temple.

But if ye had known what this meaneth, I will have mercy, and not sacrifice, ye would not have condemned the guiltless.

For the Son of man is Lord even of the sabbath day.

And when he was departed thence, he went into their synagogue:

And, behold, there was a man which had his hand withered. And they asked him, saying, Is it lawful to heal on the sabbath days? that they might accuse him.

And he said unto them, What man shall there be among you, that shall have one sheep, and if it fall into a pit on the sabbath day, will he not lay hold on it, and lift it out?

How much then is a man better than a sheep? Wherefore it is lawful to do well on the sabbath days.

Then saith he to the man, Stretch forth thine hand. And he stretched it forth; and it was restored whole, like as the other.

Then the Pharisees went out, and held a council against him, how they might destroy him (Matthew 12:1 – 14).

The debate over which day of the week constitutes the Sabbath is so divisive that congregations and entire denominations have split over it. Is it a day or is there a deeper principle to be understood? In our additional lesson text from chapter 12 of Matthew's Gospel, Pharisees who witnessed His disciples' plucking ears of corn to eat on the Sabbath confronted Jesus. Of course, the obvious question is, why were the Pharisees observing the disciples' actions instead of worshipping God in the Temple? After all, wasn't that the basis of their criticism? After addressing their complaint, Jesus went into their synagogue and healed a man with a withered hand. Jesus didn't condemn the establishment of a day for rest and worship but how the Pharisees failed to understand the big picture.

Conclusion

The Sabbath was designed as a day of rest from labors and a day on which we can best fulfill our duty to give God our undivided attention in worship and praise. Not that we aren't able to worship and praise Him any other day of the week, but on a day that we take a break from those things competing for our focus and attention, that day should belong to God. The Sabbath also conveys the importance of rest and fellowship. A necessary or worthwhile endeavor performed on that day doesn't violate the commandment. Likewise, the Sabbath is to be observed as *"a day of rest, but not a day of idleness. The time taken from secular employments must be devoted to holy pursuits"* (Exell, p. 354).

Questions:

1. Why did God establish the Sabbath? Discuss both practical and spiritual reasons for the Sabbath.

_____

_____

2. What are your feelings about establishing a set day for the Lord's worship? Why do you think this subject has caused so much division in the body of Christ?

_____

_____

3. What sorts of activities are to be enjoined on the Sabbath or any day set aside to rest and to worship the Lord? How can we keep this day Holy?

_____

_____

4. Why did Jesus refer to Himself as the Lord of the Sabbath? How did that justify the actions of the disciples and His healing the man with the withered hand?

he was lord over every thing
_____

Essential THOUGHT

"We have a duty to give God the praise and worship due His name. Praise and Worship are best given free of distractions with our focus solely fixed upon Him."

5

Exodus 20:12; 1 Timothy 2:1–3

Our Relationship Toward Authority

Central Verse

"Honour thy father and thy mother: that thy days may be long upon the land which the LORD thy God giveth thee."

Exodus 20:12, KJV

"Honor your father and your mother, so th. you may live long in the land the LORD yoı God is giving you."

Exodus 20:12, NI

Devotional Reading
Matthew 19:19–24

Key Terms

Honor – Respect that is given to someone who is admired.

Authority – Elevation, pre–emi-nence, superiority.

Supplications – 1. Need, indigence, want, privation, penury; 2. a seek-ing, asking, entreating, entreaty to God or to man.

Introduction

In Ephesians 6:2, the apostle Paul affirms this commandment is the first with a promise attached. Johr Gill in his book, *John Gill's Exposition of the Bible,* states this commandment dictates that we are to show our parents *"filial affection ...and reverence and esteem of them, and by yielding obedience to them, and giving them relief and assistance in all things in which they need it; and if honour, esteem, affection, obedience, and reverence, are to be given to earthly parents, then much more to our Father which is in heaven"* (Exodus 20:12). The disobedient are a burden to their parents, to society, and to the church.

Discussion

How does honoring parents extend life? The promise here encompasses several points. Life may be prolonged by the virtue of following parents' wise instruction; by the Lord's inclining His ear toward the prayers of parents for their children; or by the Lord's being pleased by the behavior of children toward their parents so much so that He may be inclined to supernaturally act on their behalf.

> *I exhort therefore, that, first of all, supplications, prayers, intercessions, and giving of thanks, be made for all men;*
> *For kings, and for all that are in authority; that we may lead a quiet and peaceable life in all godliness and honesty.*
> *For this is good and acceptable in the sight of God our Saviour;*
> (1 Timothy 2:1–3).

The honor, obedience, and respect that are to be given to parents extend to all persons who act in the capacity of parents or who are in the family line by blood or by marriage—grandparents, step–parents, aunts, uncles, etc. It also includes the respect, obedience, and honor to be shown to dignitaries and all others in any capacity of authority, as supported by our additional lesson texts. Paul reminds believers in our lesson texts of our duties to those in authority, just as he reminded believers in Romans 13:1 – 4 that those in authority exist because they are ordained of God and are to be used as instruments of God for our good.

Conclusion

Are we to pray for governments, leaders, and officials even if they are corrupt and abusive? Yes. J. Vernon McGee once said, *"Civil government is a gift from God, and we ought to give thanks for it and pray for it."* Even if there is only a modicum of law and order, an imperfect government is better than lawlessness, unchecked rebellion, and anarchy.

Questions:

1. *Kabad* is the Hebrew root word meaning honor. It also has negative meanings, including heaviness and burdensome. If we fail to honor those in authority, how do we become weighty burdens?

   _____

   _____

2. How do honor and obedience extend life?

   _____

   _____

3. What are the responsibilities of those in authority toward the persons under their authority?

   _____

   _____

4. If a person's parents are abusive and mistreat him or her, does that person still have the duty to honor them? What responsibility does a believer have toward someone in a position of authority who is abusing that authority?

   _____

   _____

Essential THOUGHT   "Respect for authority demonstrates our love and obedience to God."

Genesis 4:8–14; Exodus 20:13

Do Not Murder

Central Verse

"Thou shalt not kill."

Exodus 20:13, KJV

"You shall not murder."

Exodus 20:13, NIV

Introduction

Devotional Reading
Romans 13:1–9

Key Terms

Slew – To kill, slay, murder, destroy, murderer, slayer, out of hand.

Fugitive – To quiver, totter, shake, reel, stagger, wander, move, sift, make move, wave, waver, tremble.

The first murder recorded in Scripture is found in Genesis 4. Cain vented his anger, frustration, and jealousy upon his brother, Abel, and killed him. Cain buried Abel's body to hide his crime. He lied to God about what he had done. If we don't have a clear picture of Cain's character flaws from God's rejection of his sacrifice, we certainly see it in his confrontation with and subsequent slaying of his own brother. When God revealed that He knew about Cain's crime and judged him accordingly, Cain's immediate response was not one of repentance or sorrow. His only thought was that God's judgment was too harsh a burden for him to bear. He had little if any regard for God or for his brother.

Exodus 20:13 says, *"Thou shalt not kill."* Some extend the application of *kill* in principle to include slander, gossip, back–biting, and other sins which can result in *death*, in a manner of speaking, to reputations, marriages, relationships, and so on. The Hebrew word for *kill* as used here is *ratsach*. It is found 49 times in the Old Testament and refers to the intentional act of murder or taking a life. Only God can determine the worth of an individual's life. Therefore, the person who commits murder arrogantly assumes God's role.

Conclusion

There are several passages in the Old Testament where certain actions resulted in sentences of death for the guilty. Because of this, we know this commandment is not a prohibition against capital punishment or manslaughter committed in self–defense. There is nothing wrong with believers opposing capital punishment. Because of the many flaws found in the justice system, including corruption and misconduct; imperfect methods of collecting evidence; racial and socio–economic bias; and a proven history of innocent individuals being wrongly convicted, many believers are compelled to speak out against capital punishment and to work to end the death penalty.

Questions:

1. What were the circumstances surrounding the murder of Abel? Did Cain intend to kill his brother?

_____

_____

2. Discuss some examples of capital punishment from the Old Testament. Do you support or oppose the death penalty?

_____

_____

3. There have been incidents where victims of slander, gossip, and bullying have taken their own lives as a result. In these cases, are the perpetrators of these assaults guilty of murder?

_____

_____

4. How does this commandment apply to issues such as abortion, suicide, and euthanasia (assisted suicide)?

_____

_____

Essential THOUGHT "We must be careful in making judgments concerning the worth of human life."

not all this long time

Exodus 20:14; Matthew 5:27–28; Galatians 5:19–21

Avoid Sexual Sins

Central Verse

let every man have his own wi[fe]
You going to be judge

"**Thou shalt not commit adultery.**"
Exodus 20:14, KJV

if a married person

"**You shall not commit adultery.**"
Exodus 20:14, NIV

Introduction

When a person engages in sexual relations with someone who is not his or her spouse, he or she has committed adultery. The word for *adultery* used here, *na'aph* refers to marital infidelity, *usually of a man with the wife of another man*, *both were*, but also includes the infidelity of women. According to the King James Bible Online dictionary, intercourse between a married man and an unmarried woman was <u>fornication</u>. Adultery also figuratively refers to idolatry. In idolatry, someone or something ① occupies God's rightful place in our lives. <u>In adultery, someone occupies the rightful place of the spouse in the adulterer's life</u>. While all unrighteousness is sin and all sin is dangerous and destructive, sexually based sins are among the most destructive.

② "*Ye have heard that it was said by them of old time, Thou shalt not commit adultery: But I say unto you, That whosoever looketh on a woman to lust after her hath committed adultery with her already in his heart*" (Matthew 5: 27–28).

Devotional Reading
James 2:8–11

Key Terms

Adultery – Sex between a married person and someone who is not that person's wife or husband.

Fornication – Illicit sexual intercourse.

Uncleanness – In a moral sense: the impurity of lustful, luxurious, profligate living; of impure motives.

Lasciviousness – Unbridled lust, excess, licentiousness, wantonness, outrageousness, shamelessness, insolence.

Discussion

Some People say it nothing wrong with looking

During His earthly ministry, Jesus took the application of this commandment a step further. A physical, sexual act doesn't have to be committed for a man or woman to be guilty of adultery. Looking upon <u>another person in lust</u> is also <u>adultery</u>. It is the same as engaging in the physical act. This is an important application. Viewing pornography in any medium, books, magazines, or on the internet, is adultery. Fantasizing about any man or woman who is not your spouse is adultery. <u>Robbing your spouse by lavishing others with the time</u>, attention, and affection that rightfully belongs to him or her is adultery. The sin of adultery goes well beyond a sexual act—it is truly an issue of the heart, and it breaks the covenant

adultry against Husban of wife

16

relationship between husbands and wives and between believers and the Father.

(3) *Now the works of the flesh are manifest, which are these; Adultery, fornication, uncleanness, lasciviousness,*
Idolatry, witchcraft, hatred, variance, emulations, wrath, strife, seditions, heresies,
Envyings, murders, drunkenness, revellings, and such like: of the which I tell you before, as I have also told you in time past, that they which do such things shall not inherit the kingdom of God. (Galatians 5:19–21). *no sin shall enter in to the Kingdom of God*

Conclusion

Adultery is only one of the sins commonly known as *"the works of the flesh"* (Galatians 5:19). Today, the term would be *vices*. A vice is any form of *"immoral or wicked behavior."* The transgressions enumerated in this text categorize a number of sins which have but one result: *"those who practice such things will not inherit the kingdom of God"* (Galatians 5:21, NKJV).

Questions:

1. What is the connection between adultery and idolatry?
   adultery sexual involvement in Phansize

2. Why did Jesus extend the application of this commandment to include lust in absence of the actual physical act?

3. Discuss all the works of the flesh listed in our lesson text from Galatians 5.

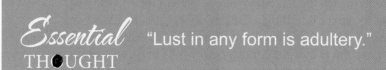

Essential "Lust in any form is adultery."
THOUGHT

Romans 12:9–20; 7:7–14

Christian Conduct

Central Verse

"Abhor that which is evil; cleave to that which is good." Romans 12:9, KJV

"Love must be sincere. Hate what is evil; cling to what is good." Romans 12:9, NIV

Introduction

Devotional Reading
Psalm 97:10–12

Key Terms

Dissimulation – Unfeigned, undisguised, sincere.

Abhor – To dislike, have a horror of.

Concupiscence – Desire, craving, longing, desire for what is forbidden, lust.

There was a feature news story about a small town in which most of the families adopted children who had been placed in the state's custody. One woman adopted a group of siblings who had been severely neglected. The children had been accustomed to eating cold cereal, fast food, and junk food—chips, candy, and sugary drinks. When the woman prepared hot, healthy meals, the children became physically ill. It took some time for their little bodies to accept nutritious food. In the same way, a person who has only fed upon a steady diet of disobedience, rebellion, idolatry, and so on has to be taught how to follow Christ and uphold his or her responsibilities in the covenant relationship with Him. *some people have not yet totally learny*

Discussion

The commandments discussed this month deal with our relationships toward others. How are we to act toward others? They lay an important foundation and show us that God's way is the right way. In establishing a covenant relationship with Israel, God gave the people the Ten Commandments so that they would know the truth of His Word above the beliefs of the heathen cultures surrounding them. God's commandments and laws served as the guidelines by which the Israelites were to pattern their lives. This enabled them to keep their part of the covenant. If they had any doubts about what was right and what was wrong, what pleased God or what displeased Him, or what was good and what was evil, the Commandments and the rest of the Mosaic Law would serve as their guide. The people were continually admonished to remember what they had been taught.

> *What shall we say then? Is the law sin? God forbid. Nay, I had not known sin, but by the law: for I had not known lust, except the law had said, Thou shalt not covet.*

18

But sin, taking occasion by the commandment, wrought in me all manner of concupiscence. For without the law sin was dead. ~no *look to*

For I was alive without the law once: but when the commandment ~brief~ *came, sin revived, and I died.* ~how shows you what was against sin~

And the commandment, which was ordained to life, I found to be unto ~God~ *death.*

X *For sin, taking occasion by the commandment, deceived me, and by it slew me.*

Wherefore the law is holy, and the commandment holy, and just, and good.

Was then that which is good made death unto me? God forbid. But sin, that it might appear sin, working death in me by that which is good; that sin by the commandment might become exceeding sinful.

For we know that the law is spiritual: but I am carnal, sold under sin (Romans 7: 7 – 14). ~get save~

Paul, in our lesson text from Romans 7, confessed that it was only through the Mosiac Law that he was taught the meaning of sin. Once he became aware of God's commandments concerning sin, he realized that he was not in covenant relationship with God, but was spiritually dead. It is only in the light of God's Word that we see ourselves as we really are.

Conclusion

Sometimes we incorrectly assume others know how God wants them to live their lives. Sometimes we forget they must be taught. Sometimes, we lose patience. Sometimes, we neglect to make the message plain or complicate it beyond anyone's understanding. When people are left to determine what is right and what is wrong on their own, they will always fall short of God's expectations. ~people in Church~

Questions:

1. List and discuss the points of Christian conduct listed in our lesson texts.

   _____

   _____

2. What is Paul communicating in our lesson text from Romans 7?

   _____

   _____

3. How do the commandments help us determine what is evil and what is good?

   _____

   _____

THOUGHT

"The Ten Commandments weren't given over the course of a few minutes. God took His time to adequately prepare the people for the challenges they were about to face."

Exodus 20:15; Ephesians 4:28; Proverbs 30:8–9;
Luke 19:1–10

Warnings Against Theft

Central Verse

Thou shalt not steal."

Exodus 20:15, KJV

"You shall not steal."

Exodus 20:15, NIV

Introduction

Devotional Reading
Leviticus 19:11–14

Key Terms

Steal – To take (something that does not belong to you) in a way that is wrong or illegal.

Poverty – The state of one who lacks a usual or socially acceptable amount of money or material possessions; debility due to malnutrition.

Riches – Wealth; large amounts of money and possessions.

This commandment teaches that we should respect the property of others. Theft is any act committed with the intent to wrongfully and permanently deprive a person of his or her property. This would include criminal acts such as burglary, robbery, shoplifting, and embezzlement. It also includes any type of scheme designed with the intent to defraud victims of money. God expects us to make an honest living.

Proverbs 6:30 teaches that people will look with compassion upon the man who steals because he is hungry. While his circumstances will be taken into account when he is judged for his crime, this verse of Scripture does not in any way support theft. There is no justification found in Scripture for stealing, no matter the reason a person steals. Though the Word of God doesn't support stealing, it does indicate that where compassion is warranted, it should be given.

Remove far from me vanity and lies: give me neither poverty nor riches;
feed me with food convenient for me:
Lest I be full, and deny thee, and say, Who is the LORD? or lest I be poor,
and steal, and take the name of my God in vain (Proverbs 30:8–9).

Discussion

Agur, son of Jakeh, equates theft with taking God's name in vain. Why? Because his actions are motivated by a lack of faith in God's ability to meet his needs. He may proclaim that he trusts in God, but his criminal activities are proof he does not. Stealing says there is no confidence in God or His promises to meet our need.

21

The biblical position on theft is further established by Ephesians 4:28. The Amplified Version of this verse says, *"Let the thief steal no more, but rather let him be industrious, making an honest living with his own hands, so that he may be able to give to those in need."* The thief is not only to repent and forsake his criminal activity but to work, making an honest living by which he may also help contribute to the needs of others.

> *And Jesus entered and passed through Jericho.*
> *And, behold, there was a man named Zacchaeus, which was the chief among the publicans, and he was rich.*
> *And he sought to see Jesus who he was; and could not for the press, because he was little of stature.*
> *And he ran before, and climbed up into a sycamore tree to see him: for he was to pass that way.*
> *And when Jesus came to the place, he looked up, and saw him, and said unto him, Zacchaeus, make haste, and come down; for to day I must abide at thy house.*
> *And he made haste, and came down, and received him joyfully.*
> *And when they saw it, they all murmured, saying, That he was gone to be guest with a man that is a sinner.*
> *And Zacchaeus stood, and said unto the Lord: Behold, Lord, the half of my goods I give to the poor; and if I have taken any thing from any man by false accusation, I restore him fourfold.*
> *And Jesus said unto him, This day is salvation come to this house, forsomuch as he also is a son of Abraham.*
> *For the Son of man is come to seek and to save that which was lost* (Luke 19: 1 – 10).

Zacchaeus was chief of the tax collectors in the region surrounding Jericho. Using his position to take advantage of others, he grew very wealthy. Wealth may sometimes be as much of a burden as poverty. Following his encounter with Jesus, Zacchaeus *"stood before the Lord and said, 'I will give half my wealth to the poor, Lord, and if I have cheated people on their taxes, I will give them back four times as much!' Jesus responded, 'Salvation has come to this home today, for this man has shown himself to be a true son of Abraham. For the Son of Man came to seek and save those who are lost'"* (Luke 19:8–10, New Living Translation).

Questions:

1. Why does Agur compare theft to taking the name of the Lord in vain?

_____

_____

2. Does Proverbs 6:30 justify theft if there is a dire need, such as poverty or hunger? How are we to view theft in such cases?

_____

_____

3. Discuss other passages of Scripture which detail how those guilty of theft or defrauding others are to make restitution for their crimes.

_____

_____

4. Why did Jesus proclaim that Zacchaeus was a *true son of Abraham*?

because he Repent. & how to make Resitution for what he had taken unlawful from other

Exodus 20:16; 23:1–3, 7

Damaging Others' Reputation.

Central Verse

"Thou shalt not bear false witness against thy neighbour." **Exodus 20:16, KJV**

"You shall not give false testimony against yo␣ neighbor." **Exodus 20:16, NI␣**

Devotional Reading
Leviticus 19:15–18

Key Terms

False witness – A person who deliberately gives false testimony.

Unrighteous – Violence, wrong, cruelty, injustice.

Testimony – Something that someone says especially in a court of law while formally promising to tell the truth; proof or evidence that something exists or is true.

Introduction

There is a difference between someone giving incorrec␣ testimony in error and someone deliberately giving false testimony with the intent that the accused is found guilty or not guilty. It is the latter that is addressed by this commandment. The results of this sin are devastating— falsely accused persons have lost their families, their livelihoods, their reputations, their freedom, even their lives. People have dubious motives for giving false testimony that aren't always apparent.

Thou shalt not raise a false report: put not thine hand with the wicked to be an unrighteous witness.
Thou shalt not follow a multitude to do evil; neither shalt thou speak in a cause to decline after many to wrest judgment:
Neither shalt thou countenance a poor man in his cause.
Keep thee far from a false matter; and the innocent and righteous slay thou not: for I will not justify the wicked (Exodus 23:1–3, 7).

Discussion

God's position on false testimony specifically and lying in general is that He hates it, so much so that He declared, *"He that worketh deceit shall not dwell within my house: he that telleth lies shall not tarry in my sight"* (Psalm 101:7). A false accusation by Potiphar's wife resulted in Joseph's being thrown into prison (see Genesis 39:7–20). In Mark's account of what happened to Jesus as He appeared before the Sanhedrin in an illegal and hastily thrown together trial, it was clear that the religious leaders were so desperate to find some reason to justify a death sentence against Him they not only sought out false witnesses but also gave false testimony themselves: *"Now the chief priests and all the council sought testimony against Jesus to put Him to death, but found none. For many bore false witness against Him, but their testimonies did not agree. Then some rose up and bore false witness against Him, saying, 'We heard Him say, "I will destroy this temple made with hands, and within three days I will build another made without hands." ' But not even then did their testimony agree"* (Mark 14:55–59, NKJV). There is no acceptable reason for telling a lie.

Questions:

1. What is the point of having witnesses swear or affirm that the testimony they are about to give is true?

   _____

   _____

2. What do our additional lesson texts say about lying and giving false testimony?

   _____

   _____

3. What were the circumstances surrounding Jesus' appearance before the Sanhedrin? What were the circumstances surrounding Joseph's imprisonment?

   _____

   _____

4. Why do you think one of God's directives toward us in Matthew 25 is the visiting of those who are in prison?

   _____

   _____

5. Have you ever been the victim (or known someone who has been a victim) of false testimony? What happened? How was your life or that person's life impacted as a result?

   _____

   _____

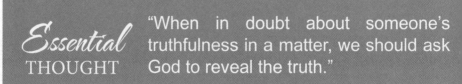

Essential THOUGHT — "When in doubt about someone's truthfulness in a matter, we should ask God to reveal the truth."

Exodus 20:17; 1 Timothy 6:5–7

Lusting For Others' Possession

Central Verse

"Thou shalt not covet thy neighbour's house, thou shalt not covet thy neighbour's wife, nor his manservant, nor his maidservant, nor his ox, nor his ass, nor any thing that is thy neighbour's." **Exodus 20:17, KJV**

"You shall not covet your neighbor's hous You shall not covet your neighbor's wife, or h male or female servant, or his ox or donkey, c anything that belongs to your neighbor." **Exodus 20:17, NI**

Devotional Reading
Romans 7:5–7

Key Terms

Covet – To desire, take pleasure in, delight in.

Godliness – 1. Reverence, respect. 2. piety towards God.

Contentment – 1. A perfect condition of life in which no aid or support is needed. 2. sufficiency of the necessities of life.

Rejected – To reject, despise, refuse.

Introduction

Though it is given as the last, this commandment exposes the sin that lies at the heart of most of the other sins addressed by the preceding nine commandments— covetousness or harboring an evil desire to have what doesn't belong to you. It implies that a person is not satisfied with the blessings God has given and so desires to have the things that belong to someone else. The person who is dissatisfied with God's provisions feels entitled to have the possessions of others. Instead of allowing himself to be ruled by the Spirit of God, he is ruled by discontentment, envy, and materialism.

Perverse disputings of men of corrupt minds, and destitute of the truth, supposing that gain is godliness: from such withdraw thyself.
But godliness with contentment is great gain.
For we brought nothing into this world, and it is certain we can carry nothing out (1 Timothy 6:5–7).

Discussion

We should be content with God's blessings. You have heard of the phrase "keeping up with the Joneses." It refers to people who strive to have the same material possessions as or live at a socio–economic level equal to or above that of others. The truth is they aren't content with what God has provided. Instead of keeping their focus upon God, they are keeping a tally of what their neighbors have. They crave the newest, latest, best, or the most expensive—they redefine success to suit their own needs. Covetousness may go beyond the desire to have what belongs to someone else. It may also include determining

26

that the person who has what another person wants doesn't deserve to have it. Can you see why it is so dangerous to allow Satan to enter into our hearts in this way? In our additional lesson text from 1 Timothy, Paul indicated such ways of thinking are perverse and corrupt.

Covetousness resulted in great troubles for Israel. Dissatisfied with the prophets and judges God had given, they demanded a king so that they would be like the nations surrounding them. The leaders of the people approached the aged prophet Samuel,

> *"And said unto him, Behold, thou art old, and thy sons walk not in thy ways: now make us a king to judge us like all the nations. But the thing displeased Samuel, when they said, Give us a king to judge us. And Samuel prayed unto the LORD. And the LORD said unto Samuel, Hearken unto the voice of the people in all that they say unto thee: for they have not rejected thee, but they have rejected me, that I should not reign over them. According to all the works which they have done since the day that I brought them up out of Egypt even unto this day, wherewith they have forsaken me, and served other gods, so do they also unto thee. Now therefore hearken unto their voice: howbeit yet protest solemnly unto them, and shew them the manner of the king that shall reign over them. And Samuel told all the words of the LORD unto the people that asked of him a king"* (1 Samuel 8:5–10, KJV).

Conclusion

Israel offered the excuse that they wanted a king because Samuel's sons were not righteous men as was Samuel, but the real reason for their demand is apparent—they wanted to be like the nations around them. Samuel was disturbed by their request, but God had long recognized the condition to the nation's collective heart. Covetousness, just like the sins of idolatry and adultery, is a heart issue. Even after Samuel made the people aware of the troubles that would befall them under a king's reign, they still desired a king. Many who desire to have the lifestyles and possessions of others can ill afford them financially, but they pursue them anyway.

Questions:

1. Why is covetousness at the root of many of the other sins prohibited in the Ten Commandments?

   _____

   _____

2. What does covetousness say about a person's relationship with God and appreciation for what God provides?

   _____

   _____

Essential
THOUGHT

"Striving to have things that don't belo
to us or which God doesn't intend for
to have can only lead to more proble
in our lives."

Exodus 20:18–26

We Have Heard God's Commandments

Central Verse

And Moses said unto the people, Fear not: for God is come to prove you, and that his fear may be before your faces, that ye sin not."

Exodus 20:20, KJV

"Moses said to the people, 'Do not be afraid. God has come to test you, so that the fear of God will be with you to keep you from sinning.'"

Exodus 20:20, NIV

Devotional Reading
Isaiah 41:10–14

Key Terms

Prove – To test, try, tempt, assay, put to the proof or test.

Nakedness – Nudity, shame, pudenda (implying shameful exposure).

In the midst – The middle or central part or point, amongst.

Introduction

God's laws were given in an awesome display of His might and power. The purpose was to reveal Himself as the True and Living God, the only God worthy of their worship. The purpose was to instill reverence for His name and ensure compliance with His commandments. The purpose was to establish His supreme right to demand their obedience.

We don't witness God's descending upon Mount Sinai every time we teach His Word, but the result should be the same—people should come away from each encounter knowing that God is worthy of worship, His name is to be feared, His commandments are to be obeyed, and He has a right to expect and demand obedience. As His presence was with Israel that day, whenever we gather in His name, He is with us, *"For where two or three are gathered together in my name, there am I in the midst of them"* (Matthew 18:20).

Discussion

Israel was so frightened by God's presence they begged Moses to speak to them instead of listening to God's commands come from the mouth of God Himself. Perhaps in light of His holiness and righteousness, they felt so condemned and ashamed that they couldn't bear to listen to Him. Perhaps the whole experience was too overwhelming. Whatever the reason, God spoke to the people through Moses from that point forward until Moses' death. He spoke to Israel through various prophets and judges throughout their history. He spoke through His Christ. He continues to communicate with us through those with whom He has entrusted with that calling. What a wonderful responsibility we have in bringing the Word of God to others.

29

Conclusion

When we teach others about God, we must do so in a way that it brings honor to His name, for He promised, *"Wherever I cause my name to be honored, I will come to you and bless you"* (Exodus 20:24, NIV).

Questions:

1. Why do you think God gave the Ten Commandments in the way in which He did?
    _____
    _____

2. Moses told the people that God had come to test them. What did he mean?
    _____
    _____

3. What can we do, as those who bring and serve as examples of the Gospel, to let others know that though God is communicating to them through us, they are indeed hearing from God as though He is speaking to them directly from Heaven?
    _____
    _____

Essential
THOUGHT

"God desires to reveal Himself to us and to communicate with us. Because of sin and shame, people may not feel worthy of God's outreach."

Exodus 21:23–25; Romans 12:18–20

The Punishment Should Fit The Crime

Central Verses

And if any mischief follow, then thou shalt give life for life, Eye for eye, tooth for tooth, and for hand, foot for foot, Burning for burning, wound for wound, stripe for stripe."

Exodus 21:23 – 25, KJV

"But if there is serious injury, you are to take life for life, eye for eye, tooth for tooth, hand for hand, foot for foot, burn for burn, wound for wound, bruise for bruise."

Exodus 21:23–25, NIV

Devotional Reading

Leviticus 24:16–23

Key Terms

Mischief – Evil, harm, hurt.

Peaceably – To make peace, harmony.

Vengeance – A revenging, punishment.

Repay – 1. In a good sense, to pay, requite. 2. in a bad sense, penalty and vengeance.

Discussion

In chapter 20 of the book of Exodus, we are given general commandments which are further expanded to cover a number of sundry laws regarding slaves, personal injury, restitution for theft and property damage, breaches of trust, seduction of unengaged virgins, keeping religious observances, and civil responsibilities. Reading these laws, it is easy to see how the Ten Commandments and the rest of Mosaic Law laid the groundwork for the civil and judicial codes of ancient civilizations then and continue to influence civil and judicial codes today.

There is no doubt that God hates sin and doesn't tolerate breaking His commandments; however, in designing the moral code and judicial system by which Israel was to govern itself, He does make provision for meting out justice that fits the circumstances the crime. In this way, we know that our God is not just some vengeful entity, but is just and loves justice. Law, order, justice, and righteousness all work together to ensure peace. According to Romans 12, as believers we should always work to find peaceful solutions to problems instead of being given to wrath and contention. And if we suffer by wrongdoing, we should allow God to take care of it: *"He will repay at the proper time and in the proper manner"* (MacDonald and Farstad, p. 1731). God fights for us. He protects us and will deal with our enemies.

Questions:

1. Why is it important that the punishment fit the crime?

_____

_____

2. As Christians, how are we to conduct ourselves when we have wronged others? How are we to conduct ourselves when others have wronged us?

_____

_____

3. Share a personal testimony on how you experienced the mercy and justice of God intervening in your life.

_____

_____

Essential THOUGHT

"We have to trust that the way God chooses to handle a situation is the best way."

References:

The J. Vernon McGee
Essential Bible Study Library
The Libronix Digital Library System
Thomas Nelson, Inc.

The Preachers Complete Homiletic Commentary
On The Second Book of Moses Called Exodus
Rev. Joseph S. Exell, M.A.
Baker Books, Grand Rapids, MI
Reprinted 2001

NOTES

NOTES

NOTES

NOTES

NOTES

NOTES

NOTES

CHURCH OF GOD IN CHRIST DOCTRINE

THE BIBLE
We believe that the Bible is the Word of God and contains one harmonious and sufficiently complete system of doctrine. We believe in the full inspiration of the Word of God. We hold the Word of God to be the only authority in all matters and assert that no doctrine can be true or essential, if it does not find a place in this Word.

THE FATHER
We believe in God, the Father Almighty, the Author and Creator of all things. The Old Testament reveals God in diverse manners, by manifesting His nature, character, and dominions. The Gospels in the New Testament give us knowledge of God the "Father" or "My Father", showing the relationship of God to Jesus as Father, or representing Him as the Father in the Godhead, and Jesus Himself that Son (John 15:8, 14:20). Jesus also gives God the distinction of "Fatherhood" to all believers when He explains God in the light of "Your Father in Heaven" (Matthew 6:8).

THE SON
We believe that Jesus Christ is the Son of God, the Second person in the Godhead of the Trinity or Triune Godhead. We believe that Jesus was and is eternal in His person and nature as the Son of God who was with God in the beginning of creation (John 1:1). We believe that Jesus Christ was born of a virgin called Mary according to the Scripture (Matthew 1:18), thus giving rise to our fundamental belief in the Virgin Birth and to all of the miraculous events surrounding the phenomenon (Matthew 1:18–25). We believe that Jesus Christ became the "suffering servant" to man; this suffering servant came seeking to redeem man from sin and to reconcile him back to God, his Father (Romans 5:10). We believe that Jesus Christ is standing now as mediator between God and man (I Timothy 2:5)

THE HOLY GHOST
We believe the Holy Ghost or Holy Spirit is the third person of the Trinity, proceeds from the Father and the Son, is of the same substance, equal to power and glory, and is together with the Father and the Son, to be believed in, obeyed, and worshipped. The Holy Ghost is a gift bestowed upon the believer for the purpose of equipping and empowering the believer, making him a more effective witness for service in the world. He teaches and guides one into all truth (John 16:13; Acts 1:8, 8:39).

THE BAPTISM OF THE HOLY GHOST
We believe that the Baptism of the Holy Ghost is an experience subsequent to conversion and sanctification and that tongue–speaking is the consequence of the baptism in the Holy Ghost with the manifestations of the fruit of the spirit (Galatians 5:22–23; Acts 10:46, 19:1–6). We believe that we are not baptized with the Holy Ghost in order to be saved but that we are baptized with the Holy Ghost because we are saved. (Acts 19:1–6; John 3:5). When one receives a baptismal Holy Ghost experience, we believe one will speak with a tongue unknown to oneself according to the sovereign will of Christ. To be filled with the Spirit means to be Spirit controlled as expressed by Paul in Ephesians 5:18–19. Since the charismatic demonstrations were necessary to help the early church to be successful in implementing the command of Christ, we therefore, believe that a Holy Ghost experience is mandatory for all men today.

MAN
We believe that man was created Holy by God, composed of body, soul, and spirit. We believe that man, by nature, is sinful and un-holy. Being born in sin, he needs to be born again, sanctified and cleansed from all sins by the blood of Jesus. We believe that ma_ is saved by confessing and forsaking his sins, and believing o_ the Lord Jesus Christ, and that having become a child of Goc by being born again and adopted into the family of God, he ma_ and should, claim the inheritance of the sons of God, namely th_ baptism of the Holy Ghost.

SIN
Sin, the Bible teaches, began in the angelic world (Ezekie_ 28:11–19; Isaiah 14:12–20), and is transmitted into the blood c_ the human race through disobedience and deception motivate_ by unbelief (I Timothy 2:14). Adam's sin, committed by eating c_ the forbidden fruit from the tree of knowledge of good and evi_ carried with it permanent pollution or depraved human nature t_ all his descendants. This is called "original sin." Sin can now b_ defined as a volitional transgression against God and a lack of con_ formity to the will of God. We, therefore, conclude that man by na_ ture, is sinful and that he has fallen from a glorious and righteou_ state from which he was created, and has become unrighteous an_ unholy. Man, therefore, must be restored to his state of holines_ from which he has fallen by being born again (John 3:7).

SALVATION
Salvation deals with the application of the work of redemption t_ the sinner and with his restoration to divine favor and communio_ with God. This redemptive operation of the Holy Ghost upon sin_ ners is brought about by repentance toward God and faith towar_ our Lord Jesus Christ which brings conversion, Faith, Justificatio_ Regeneration, Sanctification, and the Baptism of the Holy Ghos_ Repentance is the work of God, which results in a change of min_ in respect to man's relationship to God. (Matthew 3:1–2, 4:1_ Acts 20:21). Faith is a certain conviction wrought in the heart b_ the Holy Spirit, as to the truth of the Gospel and a heart trust i_ the promises of God in Christ (Romans 1:17, 3:28; Matthew 9:22 Acts 26:18). Conversion is that act of God whereby He cause_ the regenerated sinner, in his conscious life, to turn to Him in re_ pentance and faith (II Kings 5:15; II Chronicles 33:12–13; Luk_ 19:8–9; Acts 8:30). Regeneration is that act of God by which th_ principle of the new life is implanted in man, and the governin_ disposition of soul is made holy and the first holy exercise of thi_ new disposition is secured. Sanctification is that gracious and con_ tinuous operation of the Holy Ghost, by which He delivers th_ justified sinner from the pollution of sin, renews his whole natur_ in the image of God and enables him to perform good works (Ro_ mans 6:4, 5:6; Colossians 2:12, 3:1).

ANGELS
The Bible uses the term "angel" (a heavenly body) clearly anc_ primarily to denote messengers or ambassadors of God with suc_ Scripture references as Revelations 4:5, which indicates thei_ duty in heaven to praise God (Psalm 103:20), to do God's wil_ (Matthew 18:10) and to behold His face. But since heaven mus_ come down to earth, they also have a mission to earth. The Bibl_ indicates that they accompanied God in the Creation, and also tha_ they will accompany Christ in His return in Glory.

DEMONS
Demons denote unclean or evil spirits; they are sometimes calle_ devils or demonic beings. They are evil spirits, belonging to th_ unseen or spiritual realm, embodied in human beings. The Ol_ Testament refers to the prince of demons, sometimes called Sata_ (Adversary) or Devil, as having power and wisdom, taking th_ habitation of other forms such as the serpent (Genesis 3:1). Th_ New Testament speaks of the Devil as Tempter (Matthew 4:3) an_

it goes on to tell the works of Satan, The Devil, and Demons as combating righteousness and good in any form, proving to be an adversary to the saints. Their chief power is exercised to destroy the mission of Jesus Christ. It can well be said that the Christian Church believes in Demons, Satan, and Devils. We believe in their power and purpose. We believe they can be subdued and conquered as in the commandment to the believer by Jesus. " In my name they shall cast out devils;" and the work of the Devil and to resist him and then he will flee (WITHDRAW) from you. (Mark 16:17).

THE CHURCH

The Church forms a spiritual unity of which Christ is the divine head. It is animated by one Spirit, the Spirit of Christ. It professes one faith, shares one hope, and serves one King. It is the citadel of the truth and God's agency for communicating to believers all spiritual blessings. The Church then is the object of our faith rather than of knowledge. The name of our Church, "CHURCH OF GOD IN CHRIST" is supported by I Thessalonians 2:14 and other passages in the Pauline Epistles. The word "CHURCH" or "EKKLESIA" was first applied to the Christian society by Jesus Christ in Matthew 16:18, the occasion being that of his benediction of Peter at Caesarea Philippi.

THE SECOND COMING OF CHRIST

We believe in the second coming of Christ; that He shall come from heaven to earth, personally, bodily, visibly (Acts 1:11; Titus 2:11–13; Matthew 16:27; 24:30; 25:30; Luke 21:27, John 1:14, 17, Titus 2:11) and that the Church, the bride, will be caught up to meet Him in the air (I Thessalonians 4:16–17). We admonish all who have this hope to purify themselves as He is pure.

DIVINE HEALING

The Church Of God In Christ believes in and practices Divine Healing. It is a commandment of Jesus to the Apostles (Mark 16:18). Jesus affirms His teachings on healing by explaining to His disciples, who were to be Apostles, that healing the afflicted is by faith (Luke 9:40–41). Therefore, we believe that healing by faith in God has scriptural support and ordained authority. St. James' writings in his epistle encourage Elders to pray for the sick, lay hands upon them and to anoint them with oil, and that prayers with faith shall heal the sick and the Lord shall raise them up. Healing is still practiced widely and frequently in the Church Of God In Christ, and testimonies of healing in our Church testify to this fact.

MIRACLES

The Church Of God In Christ believes that miracles occur to convince men that the Bible is God's Word. A miracle can be defined as an extraordinary visible act of Divine power, wrought by the efficient agency of the will of God, which has as its final cause the vindication of the righteousness of God's Word. We believe that the works of God, which were performed during the beginnings of Christianity, do and will occur even today where God is preached, Faith in Christ is exercised, The Holy Ghost is active, and the Gospel is promulgated in the truth (Acts 5:15, 6:8, 9:40; Luke 4:36, 5:5–6, 7:14–15; Mark 14:15).

THE ORDINANCES OF THE CHURCH

It is generally admitted that for an ordinance to be valid, it must have been instituted by Christ. When we speak of ordinances of the Church, we are speaking of those instituted by Christ, in which by sensible signs the grace of God in Christ, and the benefits of the covenant of grace are represented, sealed, and applied to believers, and these in turn give expression to their faith and allegiance to God. The Church Of God In Christ recognizes three ordinances as having been instituted by Christ Himself and therefore, binding upon the Church practice.

A. THE LORD'S SUPPER (HOLY COMMUNION)

The Lord's Supper symbolizes the Lord's death and suffering for the benefit and in the place of His people. It also symbolizes the believer's participation in the crucified Christ. It represents not only the death of Christ as the object of faith which unites the believers to Christ, but also the effect of this act as the giving of life, strength, and joy to the soul. The communicant by faith enters into a special spiritual union of his soul with the glorified Christ.

B. FEET WASHING

Feet Washing is practiced and recognized as an ordinance in our Church because Christ, by His example, showed that humility characterized greatness in the Kingdom of God, and that service, rendered to others gave evidence that humility, motivated by love, exists. These services are held subsequent to the Lord's Supper; however, its regularity is left to the discretion of the Pastor in charge.

C. WATER BAPTISM

We believe that Water Baptism is necessary as instructed by Christ in John 3:5, "UNLESS MAN BE BORN AGAIN OF WATER AND OF THE SPIRIT."

However, we do not believe that water baptism alone is a means of salvation, but is an outward demonstration that one has already had a conversion experience and has accepted Christ as his personal Savior. As Pentecostals, we practice immersion in preference to "SPRINKLING" , because immersion corresponds more closely to the death, burial, and resurrection of our Lord (Colossians 2:12). It also symbolizes regeneration and purification more than any other mode. Therefore, we practice immersion as our mode of Baptism. We believe that we should use the Baptismal Formula given us by Christ for all "...IN THE NAME OF THE FATHER , AND OF THE SON, AND OF THE HOLY GHOST." (Matthew 28:19)

The Presiding Bishop, Chairman of the Publishing Board, Gener
Supervisor of the Department of Women, Contributing Writer
and the entire Prayer & Bible Band Topics Editorial Staff woul
like to thank you for your continued support.

Bishop Charles E. Blake, Sr.
Presiding Bishop

Superintendent Mark A. Ellis
Chairman, Publishing Board

Mother Willie Mae Rivers
General Supervisor,
Department of Women

Supervisor Lee Etta Van Zandt
Contributing Writer

Kimberly Freeman
Contributing Writer